How to Slay the 3-Headed Monster

Get Your Organization to *Zero Employee Turnover*
Proactive Management of your Greatest Asset - People

* * * * * * * * * * * *

"Employee turnover is the starting point. You must first stop the bleeding! Much like a trauma patient, if you do not stop the bleeding the patient will die. Everything else you do for the patient is a waste of time, money and effort."

- Clark Ingram

* * * * * * * * * * * *

DEDICATED TO

Leaders in organizations everywhere and the people whom they serve

Two are better than one, because they have a good reward for their labor. For if they fall, one will lift up his companion. But woe to him who is alone when he falls, for he has no one to help him up. Though one may be overpowered by another, two can withstand him. And a threefold cord is not quickly broken.

-　　Ecclesiastes 4:9-10,12

Foreword

by

Bob Loudermilk
Entrepreneur & Marketing Strategist

When I first met Clark Ingram at a business networking function, his career history caught my attention. He described himself as *a finance guy that got thrown into the human resources arena by the CEO, in an emergency effort to reduce employee turnover.*

During our initial visit, Clark told me about three companies that had hired him to implement the systems he had created. His track record was impressive. At each company, he was successful in dramatically reducing their turnover while increasing profits.

Clark went on to tell me about the business he planned to launch to help more organizations take better care of their most valuable resource — people.

Several months went by in which I had no contact with Clark. Then one day, while enjoying lunch at one of my favorite spots, Clark *happened* to walk in. (While I use the word "happened," Clark later explained why he believed our meeting that day was providential rather than happenstance. But that's a story for another book!)

After a brief exchange of usual pleasantries, I asked Clark a direct question. "What's keeping you from getting your business successfully launched?" Without a moment of hesitation, he explained his problem in one short sentence. "I'm horrible at marketing."

The fifteen minutes I expected to spend in casual visitation turned into over an hour of insightful conversation. Clark talked about his dreams and goals for his business, why he was launching *People Profits* and what he wanted to accomplish. As we finished up our visit and walked toward the parking lot, he casually mentioned, "Please a look at my website when you have a spare moment. And by the way, let me know if you would be interested in taking over my marketing."

A few weeks passed. Even though I was busy with other projects, my mind kept going back to the conversation with Clark. One morning, with a little time on my hands, I opened his website and started digesting some of the information. The more I read, the more I became intrigued and thought to myself, "This guy knows his stuff, but very few know him." It dawned upon me how much value Clark could bring to a huge number of organizations once they got wind of his work. The possibilities were exciting. And, like the typical entrepreneur and marketing strategist, I started formulating plans.

Clark and I continued to meet regularly over the next several months. I made it a priority to learn as much as possible about his business philosophy and the systems he had created. I also got a glimpse into his character and his passion for serving others.

The deeper I went, the more I was convinced: Clark Ingram will radically transform the lives of numerous leaders and organizations once they implement what has already proven to work!

I am very proud to recommend this book to every leader interested in making their organization one of the very best when it comes to people. Implementing these principles will bring powerful, profitable results. Expect to experience more clarity, less frustration, a better-than-ever recruiting system, and a culture of fully-engaged people.

Contents

Chronically Open Positions – The Second Head

Skills Gap – The Third Head

INTRODUCTION

The Day I Met the Monster

The first time I met the three-headed monster was in Houston Texas, while working in the finance department of an international industrial services company. The terrifying monster was trashing our greatest asset. He was firmly in control and we were bleeding out. The backbone of our organization happened to be our senior technicians and we were losing them faster than we could replace them. With the organization close to failure, we knew that we had to do something and that we had to do it fast!

One day Wes, the CEO of the organization, walked into my office in a panic. He explained how the monster was eating our lunch and why we needed to take immediate action to at least slow the monster down. At that point, we never dreamed that we could actually slay the monster. We only knew that we had to make the symptoms better…and fast. When the CEO asked me to "look into it," I reminded him, "Wes, I'm a finance guy, not Human Resources." He quickly replied, "That might be a good thing."

My charge was to fix the list of identified issues we had just discussed. I felt like David going into the valley to meet the giant, Goliath. The problem was so overwhelming. Where do I start? What are the root problems? How do we fix them?

Everybody agreed on the symptoms. And there was one solution everyone seemed eager to implement – give every person an across the board pay raise. This was not financially feasible for the company and I would later learn, to my great surprise, that it would have absolutely no effect on the monster. With 20-20 hindsight, I now realize that these people were actually feeding the monster!

Building your Plan of Attack

Are you managing your greatest asset or is it managing you?

There is a three-headed monster chewing on your greatest asset. The monster is creating chaos and using deception and distraction to damage you, your organization and your people.

When I first ventured onto the battlefield, I had no clue that the monster even existed. But he introduced himself soon after I arrived, and he easily won the first few rounds. As the fight wore on, I began to learn some things about this ferocious beast. Implementing the strategies that I have recorded in this book, the monster eventually lost his grip on our organization and our people.

Allow me to be your guide as I share how the fight started, what I learned about the monster and what finally brought about his death.

To get started, let's take a look at your greatest asset- your people. Simply put, if you are not proactively managing your greatest asset and getting the results you want then your greatest asset is managing you. If they are managing you then they are not your greatest asset – you are THEIR greatest asset.

The key word in all of this is "proactively." I see a lot of organizations who are fighting fires, running the recruiting treadmill, onboarding as fast as they can and doing it all again when they have the inevitable turnover.

If you are like many of the company leaders I have consulted, you probably feel like you spend a lot of time, money and effort on your people. And you may be questioning the Return on Investment (ROI) for all that you do.

There are so many other things you would rather spend your time on

The monster is the obstacle between your greatest asset as it is today and what you want it to be. You want to build your business, grow revenues, and expand into new geographic or sales areas. You dream of spending more time with your family and friends and enjoying your hobbies. You have personal goals you want to pursue but you keep putting off because you don't have time. You feel boxed in with no way out and no room to maneuver.

All organizations have strategies and plans for marketing, sales, finance, budgets and operations. However, when you ask them for their written Human Capital Strategy & Plan - they have nothing to offer. Almost always the response is "we try to hire the best people."

When I was first thrown into people management many years ago, we had 50+ offices scattered all over the country and we had thousands of highly skilled technicians. Having no cohesive people strategies or plans, we were a classic example of a fire fighting, reactive organization. Not surprisingly, our main symptom was high employee turnover, which was bleeding us out and threatening the very survival of our business. I was trying frantically to get my arms around what was going on.

On one particular morning, as I sipped on my coffee during my commute to work, it dawned upon me what was happening. We had a litany of symptoms because the monster was chewing on several parts of our organization. Our compensation plan was not well understood and not motivating our employees. We did not know how to recruit qualified people or even why people worked for us. We had never developed a cohesive, well thought out value-based compensation plan. Instead, we followed the outdated method of merely paying for time served.

We had received many complaints about benefits, but we had no clue as to how to make it better. We invested heavily into training our techs so that they would be highly skilled. But there was little coordination between the training department and operations. We had no workforce plan or coordination between our offices regarding our work crews, and this made us unbelievably inefficient.

Solving your turnover has to be the first step toward managing your greatest asset

Make no mistake about it - the monster does not want you to focus on solving your employee turnover problem. He knows it is the cornerstone of his power over your organization. Where could your business go if you did not have high employee turnover? Can you visualize your employee base being stable and scalable? What if you had supervisors who could handle the never-ending employee problems? Or even better, having strategies and systems in place that solved or greatly reduced the employee problems? What if your greatest asset could go from just wanting a paycheck to actually helping you build your business?

Ideally what do you want or need? You want people who are proactively looking at what needs to be done and will do whatever it takes to make the customer happy. You long for higher productivity, lower employee cost per dollar of revenue. You want people with high morale. People who have ideas and who can help you solve your pressing problems.

You know you are losing business opportunities and the cost is infinite

How much do you think you are spending not getting what you want? The answer is more than you think. The monster wants to hide this from you. He doesn't want you to know what he is costing you. Routinely the cost is double what the Owner/CEO thinks and the calculation does not include lost opportunity costs which are infinite.

Several years ago, I calculated the cost of one of my clients' turnover. In the first year it was $1 million. In the second year it was $1.2 million a year. (It always gets worse.) So he was averaging over a million dollars a year in turnover costs. His first reaction was that he thought the number was puffed by the calculation. I told him: "Fine, let's say it is puffed by 50%. So your problem is only half a million dollars! Feel better?" With frustration in his voice, he mumbled an emphatic "no". His next reaction was classic: "If I had known it was even half a million and it was fixable, I would have done something about it a long time ago."

**If you knew you had a $1 million problem
on your desk, would you do something about it?**

When I speak to clients, we always talk about the cost of recruiting, interviewing, candidate selection processes, training and onboarding. But all of these things are just the tip of the iceberg. And, they are merely symptoms. I have found that organizations with high turnover also have low productivity due to not having enough people to handle the work. Or the people they have hired are not producing at a level which would be truly efficient. Therefore, orders are not completed and at the same time you are wearing out the people you do have. You are losing revenues and profits – and the problem is getting worse.

Exhausted from fighting vs. preventing fires?

When I first start talking to a new client about their greatest asset, they usually begin by explaining how many fires their people fight on a daily basis. Each day they are running harder on the recruiting treadmill, trying to stay ahead of the turnover. They are giving a pay raise for the one and only reason of "trying to keep them". They are making promises which may or may not be kept. If the promises are not kept – the turnover gets worse.

Other organizations try jazzing up their organizational culture so people will be enthralled to work there. Yet when I speak with employees about the reasons why they work where they do - they seldom if ever talk about the "awesome culture". It is always fascinating to compare notes between what the Owner/CEO believes the employees want and what the employees actually tell me.

Your organization is mentally and physically exhausted. And that's exactly where the monster wants you. The California fires are a good example of the effects of exhaustion on an organization. The problem was that the fires went on for so long that the firefighters saw no end in sight. The physical exhaustion was bad enough, but the mental exhaustion was the real long-term problem. It is one thing to work when there is a light at the end of the tunnel. It is something else to work day in and day out and feel like you are making no progress. The ultimate problem is when you are working every day and not only do you not see progress but you believe you are losing ground. The exhaustion is now deep in your bones.

The mental exhaustion is the
real long-term problem

There is only one way out of this type of exhaustion. You need a breakthrough. But let me warn you in advance, your breakthrough will be your first glimpse of the monster and it is scary. The monster wants to blind you. He wants to deceive you into thinking that there is no permanent solution. He would lose control if you actually fixed the problem by figuring out what needs to be done to first put out the fire and then make sure it never comes back.

This is a completely different thought process. You cannot continue to do what you are currently doing. You have already proven over and over that it does not work. So, you need to break it down and start over. What presumptions are you making? What thought processes have been prevalent for so long that they are no longer questioned?

I once worked for a company that would hire twelve people when they only needed ten. Why? Because they knew that two or three of them would not even show up the next day for orientation. So, they had 20-30% turnover the VERY FIRST DAY! Why were they not showing up? Some got "better jobs" in the 24 hours after they were hired. Some just could not get out of bed on the first day. Others did not pass the drug screen. The reasons are endless and exhausting.

We solved the problem in less than a day. How? Simply, they had a thought process which needed to be adjusted and replaced with a positive process. After implementing the new process, we stopped the fire from starting.

Do you see employee turnover as just an internal problem?

Companies with high turnover do not just have an internal problem. It is also external. The word spreads. People know. Those in the candidate pool see the monster even if they don't recognize it. Most people don't want to work for a high turnover company. Why? Because they know certain attributes follow high turnover. Companies with high turnover are not going anywhere. They can't. Good people want to go on a journey. They want an awesome vision of where the organization wants to be in the future. Many of them do not even really care what the goal is.

Great people are not drawn to stagnant, low vision, no goals companies. Why? Because good people know the monster lurks there. So, who are drawn to those types of companies? You guessed it – less then great people. The attributes of a company will pull in either great, less then great or bad people.

You have to BE special to attract special people

There is another major way your employee turnover is an external problem. It affects your customers. They see the monster too, or at least the symptoms.

Here is an example. Shortly after graduating from college, I went to work for a company where I unexpectedly inherited an extra job duty due to a copy machine which was literally right outside my office door. Whenever the copier broke down most people would come to me for help. I gradually learned enough to help them about half the time. If I could not fix the issue, we would then call the technician who always left his card in the door of the copier.

I noticed that there was a stack of cards, all for the same technician. Each card had a different company name and logo, but it was always the same technician. Even though this technician had changed companies several times, we stuck with him because he knew how to fix our copier quickly. I wonder how many of these companies took the time to calculate the loss when this valuable employee left them for better opportunities. Not only did they lose an employee, they also lost business, revenue and profits. This is how the monster works. He wants to blind you to the real devastation he is causing.

You lose revenues and profits
when your people leave

How many of your employees fall into this situation either directly or indirectly? This is not limited to your sales people or service technicians, though they are good examples. The issue can be in just about any position. I have heard stories about families changing school districts so their kids could keep a certain teacher. Many times the employer may not even know they have lost a customer unless they perform an audit after the fact.

Why do these quality employees leave? Is it money driven? If the employee was asking for more money and the employer said no, would the analysis change if they factored in the loss of revenue and profits?

Every business owner has a story of the "employee who got away" and the major impact it had on their business for years. But, the loss of a customer is virtually never reviewed in such a way. They don't just lose an employee. They also lose revenues, profits and customers. I have also seen where they don't just lose the copier servicing revenue but they end up losing all the associated business in the long run. This is a huge drain for a company and is not factored into a Turnover Calculator.

The monster does not want you to be proactive. He wants to be in control and have you reacting to what he does.

Revenues and profits come to the companies with stable people

It also works in a positive way. When you slay the monster, the word gets around. People may not recognize the monster, but they will see the absence of the symptoms and will be curious as to what changed.

At one company where I worked, we had rapid success in solving their employee turnover problem. The news spread to the entire organization like wildfire. Our people were talking about how things had positively changed. They were bragging on us to family, friends and people they ran into. The news continued to spread, even beyond our organization. We were pleasantly surprised the day an entire crew, who worked at another plant decided to come talk to us. Some things that we were doing and certain issues we were solving directly resonated with them. They did not want more money. They wanted a solution to their problem. They were confident we could fix the problem they had with their current company. When they came to work for us we ended up taking over the whole plant in one day – much like the copier technician discussed above. The result was millions of dollars of revenue and profits immediately.

But the story goes on. Do you think it got around in our industry what happened? Do you think other people came to talk to us? Do you think they had already spoken to the employees who had made the move earlier? Of course they did and all they wanted was confirmation that the problem was solved. We were able to use the story for years.

Many employers fail to realize that their employees do not always leave to make more money. Most of the time they leave for reasons that cost little to nothing to solve; but cost the employer millions.

The Fundamentals of People Management

There are fundamental principles which will help you understand the monster and how he can be slayed. I have seen these principles consistently work for employers of all sizes, industries, locations and demographic groups.

What do we put first – People or Profits?

The monster likes to put you in boxes to limit your success. For example, people often debate what to put first, people or profits. I reject this question as being destabilizing. By asking the question you are putting these two areas in conflict. Choose one and the other will work against you. No matter which one you choose, you will damage the other and in the long run damage your organization.

The goal should always be a win/win with people and profits working together to benefit both. Yes, you must be creative and think outside the box. But isn't that where real value always comes from? Proactive strategies will eliminate the question and make your organization, people and ultimately your profits much stronger.

The way we designed our company logo illustrates this concept. You will notice that we have people and profits tied together with an infinity sign.

When the two are working together and not fighting each other there is no limit what the two can do. By this one simple philosophy you and your employees are on the same side. You are working together to build the organization, not creating friction between the two groups.

You can't recruit your way out of a turnover problem

The monster wants to deceive you into thinking you are making things better when he is actually walking you into a dead end. Employee turnover is inherently destabilizing as you cannot hire as fast as they can quit. All they have to do is drop their id badge on your desk and walk out the door or just not show up the next day.

You should never have to hire four before you can find one good employee

Recruiting costs are far higher than retention costs. Most retention strategies cost very little and in most cases the cost is in time and attitude not money. This fact becomes even more important as you dig deeper on this issue.

As your employee turnover continues the candidate pool will evaporate over time. This is especially true in the case of highly skilled employees.

Therefore, you have one choice:

First - Stop the Bleeding^{TM}

The monster will do everything in his power to distract and confuse you. For example, I have heard the following many times: "I have to hire four to find one good employee." Would you buy four cars in hopes that one would work? Of course not, Savvy people do their research before they buy a car they know whether the car has a good quality and reliability score. They make sure the type of vehicle fits their needs. So, if an organization finds itself in the "hire four to get one" mode, who owns the problem. Is it the candidates or the organization? Your recruiting and candidate selection process should be so highly tuned to make this a non-issue.

To be clear, this is not a matter of having layer upon layer of evaluations, personality surveys and the like. It is a matter of making the process efficient and results oriented. Like everything else, if the results are not what you want then adjust the process accordingly. Without an adjustment, you will waste an enormous amount of time and money over something that is fixable. The monster loves to pull you into spending mountains of money while not getting the results.

Increasing employee value leads to engagement

Yes, you read that right – the opposite order of what you normally hear. Conventional wisdom says that when you somehow magically increase engagement, that employees will suddenly be more valuable and productive. My research, however, shows that when you increase an employees' value first through proactive value enhancing strategies that this will then lead to engagement.

When I speak with employees they always say the same things. How do I make more money? How do I fit in? How do I make a difference? How is what I am doing helping the organization get closer to the vision? Do you hear what they are really saying? Give me a path which will benefit me and will also benefit the organization. Most employees, especially the good ones, understand profits are important both to the organization and to them.

The Power of Value Pathing^{TM}

The team at People Profits developed a system that we call Value Pathing. This is what both the organization and employee need to succeed. Proactive value-added strategies such as Value Pathing benefit both people and profits. For instance, when I explain to employees what Value Pathing is and how it works, the response is always the same. It does not matter if it is a Baby Boomer, Millennial, Gen X or anyone else. They all say, "If my last employer had given me a well-defined path, I would have never left."

The monster wants chaos and disagreement. He does not want cooperation, mutual respect and organizational success. And he will do all within his power to keep your from understanding how employee value drives employee engagement.

Pay for time served or value added?

Your relationship with your greatest asset is fundamentally economically based. The monster wants to create as much chaos as possible in that relationship.

Most organizations have what I call "Time Served" compensation plans. These plans provide for pay raises structured on the period of time the employee has been employed. For example: "After six months we will complete an evaluation and consider you for a raise in pay."

The problem is that these plans have little to no relationship to the employees' actual value to the organization.

A good to great employee will be far ahead of your average to bad employee in the first six months and will be demotivated by the typical six-month raise. They will start questioning what the future holds for them.

The average to bad employee, on the other hand, is not interested in being rewarded for their hard work and contributions to the organization. They want their reward up front.

Fewer people, individually making more money with sky high productivity

All of your positions have Key Performance Indicators (KPIs) which are linked directly to value. Tying an employees' compensation to accomplishing these KPIs, no matter how quickly they accomplish them, is the heart of a value-added approach which relates directly to organizational success.

You are now rewarding the good to great employees and giving them hope.

In addition, the Value approach will shorten the training periods which will also further organizational success. This will also spread the distance between the "good to great" versus the "average to bad".

Most companies which I come in contact with do not have an appropriate spread in compensation between these two groups. Without an appropriate spread, the result is demotivating for the good to great and a fertile ground for the monster to use the average to bad employees to damage your organization.

The monster does not want value-based compensation as it pushes him out of the process.

A 30,000 foot view
of managing your Greatest Asset

I want us to now take a couple of steps back. The following diagram shows how people management should work to maximize the value of your greatest asset. Notice that we start with a Business Strategy and Plan, coupled with a Human Capital Strategy and Plan. We then work through the seven elements of proactively managing your Greatest Asset, the Talent Results which you achieve and how those results affect your Business Results. The monster lurks everywhere and enjoys nothing more than to shred your plans and damage your results. The monster does not want to just hurt your organization. He also delights in hurting the people you work with.

Business Strategy: As provided by the owner(s) of the business. Some business strategies and plans made need to be enhanced to include the necessary information to build the Human Capital strategy.

Human Capital Strategy: The Business Strategy will be the foundation on which a Human Capital Strategy will be built. Building a Human Capital Strategy is no small feat and must be built with an eye to the business strategy and plan, company culture, ownership philosophies and characteristics of target employees. The strategies and plans must be custom built for your company. The monster wants you to focus too much on what your competition is doing versus what is best for your organization and your greatest asset.

Hypothetically, you could have two plumbing companies in buildings next to each other who are targeting the same customers with very similar business models. However, the two owners have very different values and personal philosophes which would lead to very different cultures and therefore very different strategies and plans. For instance, the candidates each company would be looking for would be very different given the values and cultural differences. The manner in which candidates would be hired, trained, deployed, engaged and evaluated would be different.

I have often seen employers who operate in this manner - doing what their competitor is doing but failing. You have to be you.

HUMAN CAPITAL STRATEGY

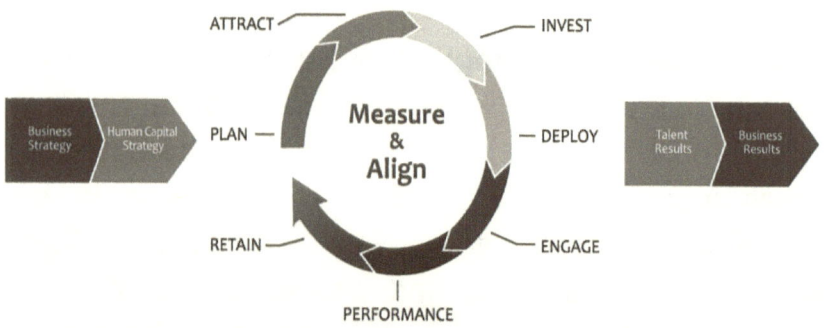

The Seven Elements of a Human Capital Strategy are extremely interactive and work together like the spokes of a wheel.

The monster enjoys confusing people and organizations into bad relationships. Most people, when looking back at their career, can remember working for companies where they "did not fit in." They probably also recall the places they worked where they felt engaged.

The real issue is to clearly define what it means to "fit in" with the company being discussed. Strategies and plans can then be formulated to increase the company's chances of attracting and hiring the candidates that fit the definition we have created.

Some organizations think that "fitting in" is somehow by chance or arbitrary. Nothing could be further from the truth. When we successfully define the criteria and implement it in the selection process, employee retention will go up and turnover will drop. As a result, all the associated time and effort and costs of employee turnover will evaporate.

Aligning all seven elements for success

Each of the following seven elements must also have a strategy which fits with the other six elements and provides for the Talent Results which the organization needs. If there are conflicts between the seven elements, you will not get the overall Talent Results you want and need.

The monster lurks throughout these seven elements doing everything to create chaos.

I have seen too many organizations trying to implement strategies and plans in each element as if it were a silo. This resulted in my having to instruct two different departments to stop what they were doing because they were cancelling each other out. I explained how we were spending money in two different areas and not getting either desired result. I then ask them to sit down together and discuss how we can get the two strategies to work together. We ended up spending less money; get better results with less effort.

This is a favorite hiding place for this three-headed beast. He thrives in working throughout the seven elements.

As you go through the seven elements think about how each are connected to the others.

Plan: these are the tactical plans of what skills we need when, where and the associated cost. This is a huge area of opportunity in most companies. Many organizations trade planning for fighting fires and thereby set the stage for future problems. Companies will copy what their competitors are doing with no review of appropriateness.

The monster does not want you to plan. Just keep focusing more on day to day and this will give him the chaos he loves.

Attract: what avenues we will use to attract the required talent. I have found over the years many companies have no idea all the avenues available, what their employer brand is or who their target candidate looks like. Seldom do they know what the target candidate is attracted by. The monster will hide avenues for recruiting but as your guide, I can help you.

Invest: analyze new skills and competencies that we must develop in our people and through what medium. Your people are your greatest asset; however they must be invested in to get the results you want. Knowing what needs to be taught and the best way to do it is not easy. Knowing how to use your investment to reduce turnover is easy once you know how to do it. The monster does not want you to plan ahead and do training ahead of time. He always wants you to merely perform remedial training.

Deploy: placing employees into the organization, establishing the employee connections and maximizing the opportunity for success. Virtually no organizations do this on a consistent basis over time and over different departments. The monster will do everything to create inconsistencies in the process.

Engage - Culture - Values: determine the norms, principles, and behaviors that make up our company and how we reinforce them in the organization. I have a very different view of how this happens compared to conventional wisdom.

The monster will always motivate the employee cancers and promote negativity.

Performance Management – Future Leaders: establish how we will measure/reward success and identify future leaders. This area and the engage area above are hard wired together. If you can get the Attract, Invest, Engage and Performance Management to truly work together, you will then see a huge, positive difference in your organization.

Retain: agree on the strategies and processes used to retain the employees who perform at the desired level. This is the final scorecard of the other six elements. The more you can get each to work well and work *together* with the other elements, your employee turnover rate and associated costs will nosedive.

Employee Turnover is the ultimate indicator of how well you are managing your greatest asset

How are your seven elements working together?

Take a look at the graphs below. Most people have results similar to the graph on top - one or two areas that are performing well while others are not doing as well. How much more effective, efficient and profitable would your organization be if the assessment results looked more like the graph at the bottom? The white area in the first graph is the areas of opportunity. The white area is where the three-headed monster lives. When you start expanding the green you force the monster out of your organization.

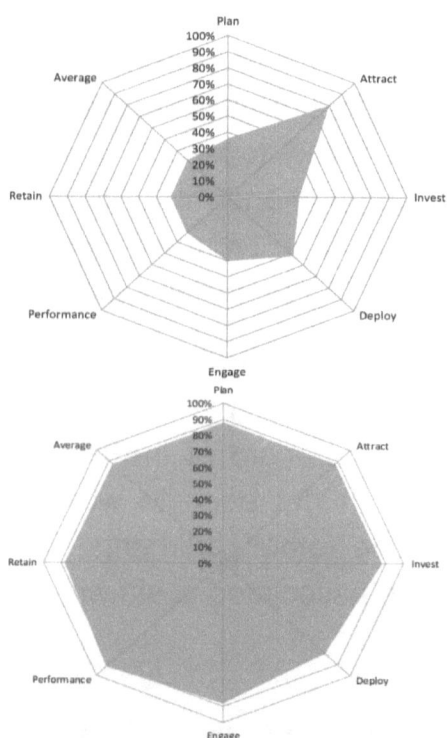

How do you manage all the moving parts?

It can feel overwhelming. You have the seven elements to deal with; large numbers of employees, daily shifts in business results, changes in business tactics, changes in the law and the list goes on. How can you keep up with it all?

The monster can use all of these variables to create chaos and maximize his damage. Knowing how he uses them and knowing how to fight back will help you move toward controlling your turnover and proactively manage your greatest asset.

Organizations do not know how bad something is – until they start to make it better

A great analogy of how to pull all of these pieces together is a cooking recipe. I know how to boil water, warm up a bowl of soup and maybe a few other things. But I would never try to bake a cake. Why? When you bake a cake every ingredient serves a purpose, and every ingredient has to be in perfect balance for the cake to turn out right. If you try baking a cake using a recipe that asks for a pinch of salt, and you put in three pinches instead, you are not going to like the result.

Individual decisions made from an agreed – on philosophy, values and strategy

Business Owners, CEOs, and General Managers routinely ask how I am able to significantly reduce employee turnover. They are looking for a magic bullet. They are thinking in terms of a one shot – "one and done" solution. Trust me, when you start talking about something like employee turnover there is no magic bullet.

Back to our analogy, the cake must be made precisely, per the recipe, no mistakes, no variations or it will not be what you want. To further the analogy, you have to decide what kind of cake you want to make. Is it going to be chocolate, Italian wedding or your personal favorite, whatever that might be? Each recipe is different for each type of cake. In addition, how big is the cake going to be? The "recipe", which are your strategies, plans and processes, will be formulated to solve the specific employee turnover ISSUES your organization is having. Don't miss that point. You have issues with an "s". That point alone leads you to a recipe rather than a magic bullet.

There are a couple of bakeries close to where I live. They sell cakes, pies and other yummy things by the slice all the way up to a full cake or pie. It is what they do. Regardless of what I buy there, it is always delicious. If I were to ask them for a custom cake, maybe a slight variation, I have no doubt it would be great. Baking will never be one of my strengths. I have never baked a cake and have no immediate plans to. In the words of Clint Eastwood, "a man has to know his limitations." However, I have skills and experiences in another important area.

I served as VP of Human Resources for four different companies, in four different states, and four different industries. The recipe for solving each of their employee turnover problems was widely different. The root problems, organizational structure and culture, demographics, organizational goals, and innumerable other criteria were different. What the organizations were doing well and not so well varied. What needed to be enhanced, tweaked, completely overhauled and created from scratch depended on the situation. My job was to create the recipe and help with the process. Each time, I succeeded in creating a recipe which reduced employee turnover dramatically.

The monster must be hit and hit HARD on all fronts. You cannot truly hurt the monster by hitting him here and there a couple of times and expecting it to work. To manage your greatest asset, you must implement a cohesive and consistent strategy.

The low hanging fruit of employee turnover

The monster invariably leaves low hanging fruit; fruit that can be picked immediately. You need to know what to look for and how to pick it.

Low hanging fruit always exists and quickly monetizes the effort on the part of the organization. There are issues which you can quickly identify and solutions that can be implemented immediately or in a short period of time. In each case, the solution costs little to nothing and the benefits are immediate.

There are many examples of what this low hanging fruit could be and the potential solutions. But remember, the low hanging fruit is always the symptom, not root cause. These are secondary symptoms that have been created by the root causes, the employees or by the organization incorrectly trying to deal with their employee turnover. Many times these are policies and procedures which have been around for a long time and are "how it has always been done".

The solutions are generally not earth shattering

I once worked with a large service company which had a particular department with a major problem. The manager woke up every day "in the hole" (her words). Imagine waking up every day "in the hole". How miserable would THAT feel?

She explained to me how she woke up every morning to several text messages from employees who were sick or could not come in for various reasons. She said that she started every day being 4-5 people "in the hole".

During the first 3-4 hours of each day, she and her staff would get on the phones and call people they had on a list to see if they could come in. The best case scenario was one of these people would say yes and they normally would get to the company by 11:00 in the morning. Her department had two key projects which had to be completed - one in the morning and another in the afternoon. The project in the morning was always very difficult due to the missing people.

The monster had a good grip on her and her department. Every day was a miserable experience.

I have seen other organizations use temporary agencies and pay a upwards of a 35% premium on the hourly rate to get people. In addition, the best situation every day was being down 4-5 people for four hours a day. Their day started at 7:00 AM and the first group of called in people would arrive at 11:00 AM or later. Obviously, productivity for the morning project was crashing and burning.

The solution I recommended cost nothing. It changed their process somewhat; but more importantly was the timing. The manager woke up fully staffed every day. Her staff could work on other things and everyone arrived on time. The employees received a full day shift; the manager had full productivity throughout the day, bonus productivity due to her staff not having to spend half a day calling people and none of the chaos.

Can you imagine the differences in the attitude, morale and engagement of the department and the manager?

This is a good example of how one of the effects the three-headed monster was having on the organization and how it was solved. In this one area the monster was not only wounded, but killed.

Discussions on each of the three heads

In the following pages, we will detail some issues regarding the three heads of the monster: Employee Turnover, Chronically Open Positions and Skills Gap. These discussions are the tip of the iceberg of topics that can be reviewed to help you slay your monster.

Employee Turnover

The First Head

Employee turnover eats culture and strategy for breakfast

When I first encountered the three-headed monster I knew nothing about him. I knew what I wanted - great people, making good money, enjoying their work, happy with the organization and the organization making money. I wanted employees who would say great things about us and most importantly would stay with us. I also knew if we did not solve our employee turnover problem we would fail as an organization. In other words, we would be faced with bankruptcy, being sold or merged with another company which was against both my CEOs and my desires.

In view of the challenge before us, my quest began by talking to people to get their take on what we were facing. The first obstacle I ran into was the following statement: "40% employee turnover is average for our industry – that's just the way it is."

Resigned defeat is always the number one symptom I encounter regarding employee turnover. I have heard variations of the above quote from numerous industries, states, and sizes of organizations. The organization recounted their past failed attempts to slay the monster.

In every case the past efforts have been focused on the symptoms - not the root causes. As you know, treating symptoms not only does not fix the problem it creates additional problems.

At this point, I did not know the monster existed but I had already identified a chink in his armor. What I noticed was found in the quote above. I zeroed in on their use of the word, "average" and realized that there were organizations doing better and in some cases much better.

As with any bell curve, there are always plenty people grouped at the average. The down side is truly scary - but the upside is amazing. So how do you move from the average to the upside?

Simply, I have never found an organization which somehow just got lucky and had low employee turnover. They all had to understand their unique problems and how to manage the issues to get the results they wanted. Logically, there was a force out there which was impacting the organization. Where was it coming from?

This was the first time the monster revealed himself to me. While I didn't get a good look, I sensed that there was something out there I was fighting.

**Low employee turnover happens
when we manage for it**

But if it was a monster I was fighting, then it was not a matter of just stabbing it a couple of times and moving on. The monster had to be slayed and I had to be vigilant to confirm the monster was not coming back or would be met with strong resistance every time it reared one of its' heads.

There are many organizations whose goals are to just slow it down or to make the situation a little better then what it was. But, could the monster be slayed and kept out of the organization going forward? The bell curve gives us the answer. Other organizations had done it and also showed it was sustainable. But, how did they do it and how was it sustained?

After some research, I learned these organizations had certain things in common. A certain philosophy, which successful manufacturers have subscribed to for many years.

The organizations with low turnover always understand:

1. The goal must always be ZERO – within the context of your organization

2. They address the REAL root causes of their turnover – they work past the symptoms

3. Substantive changes must be made to ALL issues – cosmetics will not work

4. There are no silver bullets and even when it is better – it can come back

You can have an amazing culture and a great business plan and strategy. But, if there are issues running your people off at a high rate, your culture and strategy will fail. The first issue was for me to recalibrate my brain.

What is the new goal?

Zero Employee Turnover –
an organizational philosophy

Years ago, many manufacturing companies were fighting another monster. They were spending lots of money on their production lines. The ideas, systems and processes brought by Constant Improvement, Lean Manufacturing and Six Sigma were rejected as being unrealistic. Many people thought about the manufacturing process the same way we think now about employee turnover. "As long as we are close to the industry average we're okay".

But something changed, when Lean Manufacturing, Six Sigma and Continual Improvement philosophies were engaged. Results could now be measured. People saw a difference and manufacturing organizations recalibrated their thought processes. Those who failed to do this were left behind and became dinosaurs of a previous era.

One of the companies I worked for had a manufacturing unit which had ZERO TOLERANCE for:

- Manufacturing rejects
- Customer Returns and
- Waste - among other things

Quickly, the new goals within the manufacturing process were ZERO. They slayed their monsters which were costing them BILLIONS and they have managed to keep those monsters away. Why can't these same principles be used to slay the employee turnover monster attacking so many organizations today?

The first problem is in dealing with the prevailing conventional wisdom. The employees and managers I worked with were resigned to our employee turnover being near or over the industry average. They made it clear they did not believe anything could be done to make it better. They pointed out our major competitor had the exact same problem.

One employee pointed out a company which did not directly compete with us but were in the same industry. "THEY don't have any turnover!" Another employee asked, "How and why can they do it and we can't?"

This was our FIRST STEP on the quest of zero employee turnover – the question of why it couldn't be done.

Our company production philosophy demanded management of the production line to GET AS CLOSE AS POSSIBLE to zero in multiple areas. They would manage it every day and continuously thought of new ways to strive for zero. However, we also had a resigned acceptance of employee turnover as long as it is close to the industry average. Little to no thought or effort was spent on GETTING TO ZERO.

We need the same attitude regarding employee turnover as we have with waste and rejects

Would the same management fundamentals used in manufacturing convert to employee turnover? The short answer is yes. I have seen it over and over. Taking the basic goal of continuous improvement coupled with fundamental management principles. As in manufacturing, it is not one and done. It is a long-haul process.

Clearly, we had divergent goals within the organization and our current employee turnover philosophy had to be scrapped. The new philosophy would be in line with our friends in manufacturing. The new goal was ZERO EMPLOYEE TURNOVER and we would now manage for that goal.

With this new goal and philosophy firmly in mind we had engaged the fight with the three-headed monster. This gave us renewed hope. Other companies were being successful in killing the monster and other relatable monsters had been slayed. Why not us!

My next logical step was to determine how to start the PROCESS of getting to ZERO employee turnover. This new quest consumed me.

I made a strong resolve to track down the monster and do away with him…forever.

Measuring Employee Turnover

The monster wants to sow random chaos into your organization. Continual Improvement has a fixation on measuring everything about the process. This reminded me of Peter Drucker's' famous quote:

"You can't manage what you can't measure"

The converse of Peter Drucker's famous quote is also correct. If you can measure it, you can manage it. So, I started looking into what measurements were available on employee turnover with little hope of finding anything. After much searching, I was relieved to find that much of the information I needed was readily available in our payroll system.

The many facets of employee turnover are infinitely measurable

The initial information which I received was standard payroll reports which allowed me to begin analyzing our employee turnover. I have since learned the vast majority of organizations have these reports already in their payroll systems and are readily available. I have also learned many organizations do not use these payroll reports to the extent they should be.

With these reports, the first order of business was to determine the annual cost of our organizations employee turnover. I used a fairly typical Employee

Turnover Calculator. The amount being spent on turnover floored both me and my CEO. I have since learned it is always an unpleasant surprise to the Owner/CEO when the true cost of turnover is finally revealed. Everyone always knows it was bad; but NOT THAT BAD.

As discussed earlier, when you have a $1 million problem it is easy to justify what it takes to solve it.

Once we knew how bad the monster was chewing on us, we could move on to analyze how the problem was being created and continuing.

Our payroll system also had other standard reports which provided much insight into the employee turnover for the last few years. Additional analysis provided answers as to the WHAT, WHEN and WHO questions. The reports also pointed us in the direction of why. The WHY will only come into focus with additional discussion with managers, employees and even ex-employees, if they are willing to cooperate.

We were now getting a good, long look at the monster. A much better idea of where and how he had been hurting us.

I was stunned at how much information was readily available. Everything we needed was already being measured!

Many organizations are not even aware of the reports which are available from their own systems. However, it takes someone who knows where the information is and how to use them to correctly diagnose the problems. The three-headed monster will not give up that information easily or quickly. He knows that with the proper information, we can severely hurt him. So he will do everything he can to throw us off track. He will hide, conceal and distract us from what the real root causes are.

Determine the real root causes

What was actually causing our turnover? Was it the same reason for our Chronically Open Positon and Skills Gap? Were the root causes the same for all three or different for each one?

In the beginning, I thought in terms of THE CAUSE. I thought we would find and solve this one problem and slay all three heads of the monster. I now know that it is multiple issues with one or two taking the lead FOR EACH HEAD. I also know the heads of the monster are connected but each head has some degree of autonomy. Therefore, the solution may or may not be directly related to the other heads.

I have also since learned each organization is different. Scary?

As you think of the monster, where would you attack? The three heads or the body? Attack one of the heads and the other two heads will eat you for breakfast, which means you just fed the monster.

The naysayers in the organization will again say "it is what it is". Attack and slay the body and all three heads will die quickly. The problem, however, is that the body is not just one issue. It is multiple issues, combined together.

**The body of the monster is the root cause
and the heads are the symptoms**

Discovering the actual root causes of our employee turnover was challenging but ultimately very rewarding in both money and employee engagement. However, most of the initial discussion was focused on symptoms because:

1. Symptoms are always grossly over reported
2. There were hidden agendas driving me to address the symptoms
3. People were not trained/experienced to sift through the symptoms
4. It would have been easier to deal with symptoms

The monster wanted me to attack its' heads as it could have easily eliminated me.

There was a predisposition in the organization to deal with those symptoms. The employees would have been happy for me to address the symptoms as it would have rewarded their hidden agendas.

I have learned in every single case, one of the reported symptoms will be compensation. And in most cases, compensation will be the lead symptom.

The cornerstone of reducing our employee turnover was to determine the true root causes and identify the strategies and processes to address each one. Each strategy was developed with the understanding that the process would have to continue over time and would be revised when root causes changed and more information emerged.

We learned that issues would change as we made progress in one area. And as we made changes, the monster was clever in making changes in what he was doing. But we also understood we were at last attacking the very body of the monster.

Finding the real root causes has to be more then exit interviews. There must be a multi-channel process to determine and confirm the root causes.

There are five strategies to get to the truth:

1. Confirm the exit interview procedure is not STEERING the employee
2. Review each exit interview for PLAUSIBILITY
3. Determine high turnover departments for EXTRA SCRUTINY
4. Develop CONFIDENTIAL communication channels to the EX-EMPLOYEE
5. Develop similar channels from SOURCES CLOSE to ex-employees

Each organization will have different problems to different degrees. It is imperative each root cause is identified and eliminated. You will not fix your employee turnover problem until you correctly identify the root causes. When you do, you finally KNOW your monster, and he is easier to slay.

The root causes of our turnover led us to a question we did not know how to answer

The Magic Question:
What are the 5 reasons our employees work for us?

Such a fundamental question, yet we had no clue. While we had our own ideas, we had no confirmations from the people who counted. Numerous organizations struggle with that simple question. Most of the reasons I am given are general and vague. A 15-30 minute conversation with your guide will lead to five specific reasons which can then be confirmed with the employees.

The five reasons are different for each company and are very organizational specific. The more you know about your employees, the easier it is to effectively attack the monster.

Before the strategies can be developed we will have to validate the reasons. The organization needs to interview a few employees. I always suggest you start with your very best and work down through some average employees; but don't forget the bottom third.

Good employees want an opportunity –
bad employees just want a paycheck

All different levels of employees will help validate the five reasons. But they will also help identify the reasons why the bottom third also come to work for you and will show you the antithesis of your five reasons. Knowing what attracts the bottom third is very important.

In every case, employees will provide answers which will surprise the Owner/CEOs and provide a much clearer idea. One of the issues which will become clearer will be how much compensation is NOT a driver.

If hiring is paying someone $x/hour – they are a commodity and NO ONE wants to be a commodity

The final five reasons will be the cornerstones to recruit and retain employees going forward. The five reasons will also help us decide who will NOT be recruited or hired. The reasons were always there – but they needed a guide to help identify and understand what they are and how to use them.

Our five reasons led to solving a huge problem for us. One of the first symptoms was the need to hold on to bad employees because we needed "warm bodies" to perform the work. So no matter how unproductive they were, we kept them around. When we started making progress with our employee turnover we were able to quickly start shedding the warm bodies.

Over the years this concept has led me to a basic understanding of the difference between good and bad employees:

Always be very open to the five reasons as they can be all over the board. For one company when I was the Vice President, we were able to attract a large number of our competitors' employees. They generally came to work for us for the same amount per hour which they were making at the other company. We would review how much they made and what skills and experience they had and how much we would pay someone for those skills and experience. Seldom did we have a major problem with their hourly rate.

So why were they coming to work for us? One of the major problems which this classification of employee dealt with was problems in the field. Employees in this classification would have daily problems with a job and getting the result the customer was requiring. The company I worked for had an excellent Technical Support department. They had over 50 years of combined experience and were just a phone call away from the technicians in the field.

Have you ever been in a position where you wished you had a lifeline a phone call away?

Our competitors did not have this in place, so their technicians were on their own to figure it out. Having a lifeline to solving their problems meant the world to both newly-hired and even senior technicians. For this reason, they were not concerned about a pay raise as they were about reducing their stress by getting a quick solution to a major problem they had.

With every organization there is at least one issue the monster is able to hide in and use - the issue which management will not deal with for some reason. This one issue could be a springboard making all the other root causes harder to eliminate.

Which employee group is hearing, "I want you to stay?"

Every organization has good and bad employees. If you do not discipline the bad employees and fail to reward the good ones, you will end up with a lot of bad employees. And, tragically, you will be feeding the monster. Simply, the bad will stay and the good will leave over time.

The good news is the reverse is also true. If you discipline the bad employees and reward the good ones you will end up with fewer bad employees and more good employees. In the second scenario, some of the bad employees will become good employees because they see the rewards.

Your employees know the good and bad employees. How you deal with each will determine who will stay.

When you solve your employee turnover problem you gain flexibility in dealing with your less productive employees. When you have high turnover you are forced to keep people you know are not productive because you need warm bodies.

When you have an employee who is not productive or is marginal – what do you do? Most companies will allow the problem to continue and address it only when a problem surfaces.

I have always advocated a procedure with agreed upon objective behavior improvements and a timetable.

I am going to be proactive rather than waiting around for another problem to surface. I have learned that employees will only take action when they know you are serious.

One of the companies I worked with would "retread" previous employees. The employee turnover was so bad that they began to search for previous employees and rehire them because they needed warm bodies. They would rehire them over and over. Once we solved the turnover problem we had a discussion about "retreads". I asked the branch managers how many times they rehired someone and saw it actually work in the long run. The managers agreed that retread hiring rarely worked.

After some discussion, it was revealed and agreed upon - employees who were rehired back the first time would work out at a much higher percentage. Those employees would recognize the fundamentally positive work environment. However, employees who were rehired more than once would fail 99% of the time.

From that date forward, we implemented a policy of only rehiring someone one time. This sent a message to everyone. We would give people a second chance but would not be taken advantage of.

THAT issue which springboards your employee turnover

When we first started talking about making changes to the organization to reduce our turnover we started running into lots of reasons why we could not make the necessary changes. I have found every organization has THAT issue - an issue or issues which have not been resolved and therefore continue to create turnover for years.

THAT issue can be lots of things; but they all have one thing in common. Everybody knows about it, talks about it; but, it is ignored by management. The monster will attack you when you start implementing changes as it does not want you to face the real problems.

For instance:

1. The owners' brother-in-law is the organization's worst supervisor and refuses to be coached.
2. Management behavior is not aligned with their words.
3. A supervisor steals their employees' ideas and presents them as their own.
4. Favoritism in infinite forms.
5. Supervisors who say they have an "open door" – but make it clear by their actions they are not really listening.

I know of one company that sent out a memo detailing how company profits had hit another record. The very next communication which went out from corporate announced a hiring and pay increase freeze for the foreseeable future. Just imagine how those communications and their timing went over with the company's "greatest asset".

Favoritism will be rampant whenever there are less then objective criteria for managing the greatest asset. As objective measures are inserted into the system, the managers who are the greatest abusers of favoritism will scream the loudest. The other group who will complain are the employees who are receiving the benefits of the favoritism. How do you think the rest of the greatest asset will respond?

*Employee evaluations should be
high on objective criteria*

Sometimes it is not favoritism. It can also be a case of righteous misanalysis. On a production line we inserted a scanning process which told us in objective results who were the most efficient workers. The managers were dumbfounded. Some of the results were in direct conflict with the subjective opinions of the supervisors.

The reason why management does not confront the issue is as varied as the issue itself. I have seen companies who when confronted with the objective facts still did not make the appropriate changes. Again, the reasons why were varied and generally not for the best of the company.

As we moved through our analysis of our employee turnover, I eventually encountered what I consider to be the saddest form. People who should have never been hired in the first place because they did not meet the target criteria and were soon gone. The monster is an expert at distraction and chaos which lead to bad decisions.

How to prevent the saddest form of employee turnover

Finding the right people who will stay with you starts with making sure the organization and the job applicant are on the same track.

Many times when working with an organization, I see employees who should have never been hired. It is often due to the organization not identifying their target candidate criteria or making unwise exceptions to their own criteria.

The excuse is always the same: "We need bodies NOW".

The candidates make it even worse as they do not have their criteria for what they are looking for in a job. They say: "I need a job – now."

It will just be a matter of time before the employee will decide to move on or the organization will decide that they "don't fit in". This is amazing to me. They decide six months later they don't fit in?

The organization should have known at the time of the application review or the interview they did not meet the criteria. Both the organization and the employee are hurt for the same reason and it is sad.

The organization and the candidate are trading a short-term problem by creating a long-term problem.

In these cases, organizations have done a disservice to the employees by hiring them and to the organization by setting up a future problem which will always have to be resolved later.

Here is the real question to be addressed:

What does our ideal candidate look like and how can we find enough of them to fill our positions?

Once you have identified your candidate criteria, finding quality people becomes a lot easier. Now it is a matter of finding the appropriate sources and determining how you get the attention of the candidates. What are the candidates' criteria which they are looking for?

The better your employees – the fewer you will need

Most candidates are not looking just for what the job is going to be over the next six months. The monster never wants anyone thinking long-term because he loses power.

The better candidates are looking how they will fit in, grow and be challenged in the future. They are looking for A PATH and they expect the organization to provide it.

Every company I have worked with has struggled with this issue of how the employee will be challenged beyond what they are being hired for originally. Employees want a clearly defined, well thought out path including the training, experience and accomplishment standards for success. When an organization has this as a recruiting tool they will be able to recruit, hire and retain the type of employees they want and need.

Good people bring you better people.
Bad people bring you worse people

The fundamental truth of good and bad employees affects your employee turnover in so many ways. So how do you maximize the good and minimize the bad?

1. Being able to spot the difference at the time of hire
2. Fully understanding the multi-level cost of bad employees
3. Knowing what is seen as an "opportunity"
4. Warm bodies are always bad in the long run

Every employee you hire will have weaknesses, which handled appropriately is an opportunity.

I have seen many companies who are fully aware of the weaknesses of each employee. Yet they seldom take direct action to strengthen those areas.

How your employee turnover affects your good employees

After they are hired, employers can always identify the employees in the "good" and "bad" groups. At that point, many of the "good" employees have passed you by. How many times have you interviewed someone and wanted to hire them, but they take another job before you make your offer? To fill your positions, you end up hiring people who are not your first choice.

How long does it take for you to identify the new "bad' employee? When they are late the first day? They fall asleep in training? They won't stay a little late to finish a job? Quality is not a priority? They are already costing you dearly. All of these issues will manifest themselves in the first six months of employment; therefore, reducing turnover in the first six months is critical.

Good employees can smell an opportunity! Opportunities come in all shapes and sizes. Many employers do not have a good handle on the employee opportunities which already exist in their organization. The organization doesn't know how to package them so the good employees can clearly see the opportunity, the required steps and their reward.

Good employees love challenges and want to be in the middle of overcoming a challenge. Bad employees run from challenges. Bad employees see challenges as more work and are ill equipped to help you and your good employees solve the challenge.

Employers struggle to recognize the synergy between profits and employee opportunities

Good employees will receive multiple offers and will accept the one they see has the best long-term opportunity, not necessarily the one with the most money up front. Many times a good employee will look beyond the money and look for the opportunity which best fits their LONG-TERM SITUATION.

Did you catch that? If they are making decisions based on the long-term then they are inherently inclined to not leave, therefore further helping your elimination of turnover.

As my fight with the monster continued, the most disheartening thing was to talk to good employees who I KNEW were good employees. Employees who would do anything for the company – work late, demand quality and help train new employees. When I spoke to them there was a pervasive hopelessness created by the employee turnover.

The creed of the fatalist - "It is what it is" and therefore cannot be changed. There may be some talk about what is being done to reduce employee turnover but they are not seeing it.

This hopelessness is a cancer on your greatest asset and your culture. Have you been around when one of those good employees do leave? The morale of everyone else plummets and the underground chatter is deafening. Everyone else dusts off their resume again.

Hopelessness is infinitely expensive
and
excitement is infinitely profitable

However, hopelessness can be turned around quickly if the issue is taken straight on. If the root causes are correctly identified, strategies and plans developed and implemented successfully, progress will be evident almost immediately. It is the good employees who are the first to jump in and help. They want it to be better. I have seen this many times at various organizations.

The hopelessness starts to be dispelled when:

1. The plans are announced and they make sense to middle management and the employees
2. The employees see the first concrete positive change
3. When the changes first begin to affect the individual employees work day

During the implementation stage, the good employees will sense the change in the direction and they will see the first positive results. It will be exciting – which is the opposite of hopelessness. At this point, employees will start jumping on the bandwagon. They don't want to hear the negative stuff anymore. Now the horizon is seen as a place even better than it is now.

When you are mired in hopelessness the horizon is not seen as any better and in most cases will be seen as something that will be even worse.

When you have traded hopelessness for excitement there are certain benefits:

1. Employee turnover will go down
2. You will gain control of your Greatest Asset
3. Recruiting will become easier if managed correctly
4. Productivity and engagement will go up

I have seen this over and over. This is when it gets fun and exciting. You now have much more control over your greatest asset. You can use to springboard to growth in both revenues and profits.

The monster can be slayed, it can be better; you can have the great employees you want. Slaying the first head of the monster has already severely hurt the second head. Now let's slay it too!

Chronically Open Positions

The Second Head

Slaying the first head
will weaken the second head

By reducing your turnover, the number of positions coming open is less. The number of positions staying open will also be reduced. Therefore you are recruiting less and thereby saving a lot of money. Your manpower will now be open to doing more important things.

But beware! The monster may still be chewing on you. How many open positions do you have? How many are just sitting there with no real applicants as the applicants are not close to what you really want?

The monster keeps forcing you to push the standard down. You are hiring people who you are not enthusiastic about. But you need people!

It seems hopeless as you watch the competition get the better people while you scratch your head and wonder how they are doing it. You can't afford the benefits, the perks or anything else.

There has to be a way out; but you just don't see it.

As with employee turnover we are going to start with the fundamental issues and attack the body of the monster so we can slay the head.

Have you ever thought…

"I can't find great employees,
or even good employees!"

Let's review some earlier questions and add a couple of new ones:

1. Who are you as an employer?
2. What is your reputation in the broad workforce?
3. What do you want it to be?
4. What are five reasons why someone would want to work here?
5. What do your target candidates look like – in detail?

Some of these questions have already been tackled. But some have not. Let's look at number two and ask the question slightly different:

What is your reputation as an employer in the candidate pool?

Some of the people in the candidate pool have already worked for you. What do you think they are saying about you?

This was one of the biggest problems I had every time I started fighting the monster at a new organization. Think about it. An organization which has high turnover will inevitably have a bad reputation as someone to work for. Candidates will tell each other: "Go apply at Acme Widget – they will hire anyone."

The monster is living large!

Identity: Who are you as an employer and who are your target candidates?

Would you rather have them say: "If you go apply at Acme Widget – you better have your A game face on."

As we fought the monster, I knew we were winning when the standard of the candidates coming in to be interviewed kept going up. No one showed up in flip flops and shorts. We were turning people away at the door because they were clearly not ready to interview with us. We would respectfully inform them that their interview had been either postponed or cancelled due to how they were presenting themselves.

The monster HATES when the standard goes up

As we discussed earlier, most organizations have no idea what any of the answers are. With a simple 30-minute coaching session, I have been able to help companies get a good start on their Employer Brand and recruiting strategy.

Every organization is special in multiple ways, but most organizations are too close to the forest to see the trees. They have lost track of who they are and what makes them special.

When you are looking at buying a car do you want to hear "it will get you where you want to go"? Or do you want to hear about the features which are exactly what you are seeking?

When reaching out to a candidate, it is the same issue. The good candidates are looking for certain things. Are you responding to their desires or just paying them $x an hour?

You need to build an employer brand and marketing scheme which will resonate with the best people in your industry, geographic location and employee demographics.

The monster wants you to think that you must have more and more. Spend more money, have more stuff.

My battles with the monster have proven one thing over and over – take what you have now, laser focus on who your candidates are, who you are as an employer and how they would be a great fit for your organization.

Right now you don't know what it means. The monster is hiding it from you. You need someone to help guide you to the answer.

Great employees are special and want to work somewhere special

The next step is to make sure you are communicating to the right person. There is no difference between selling someone as a customer and selling a candidate on why they want to work for you.

So how do we know we are talking to the right person? What does your target candidate look like? This is a very broad question involving education, skills, values, goals, personality - among many other things. This description changes somewhat for every position but is manageable.

There are clues within your own organization which will help you find this description without it being burdensome.

Many organizations spend time recruiting and hiring people whom I would have never even interviewed, based on what I could see on a resume. They simply were not in our target group. This is how the monster wastes your time and resources. It is also how he destroys your reputation.

Don't let the monster rush you into a bad hire

The monster will deceive you into believing you do not deserve great employees. So, once you know who you are, start figuring out what a great employee is looking for and what they are NOT looking for.

There is a huge difference between what a bad or even good employee wants in a job and what a great employee is looking for. So, what does a great person want in an organization?

Great employees will ask the following questions:

1. What makes your company special as an employer?
2. Where are you going as an organization?
3. Why should I believe we can get to the goal(s)?
4. How am I going to make a difference?
5. Am I going to fit into the culture and values?

You may be wondering: "What if I give them the wrong answer? Won't I lose them?" The beauty of this situation is that the only "wrong" answer is to describe your organization incorrectly. If you have developed your Employer Brand correctly, identified your Target Employee, are focused on those people and can show the candidate how they will make a difference – you will have plenty of quality candidates.

Quality people always have jobs but many of them are not happy. They work for organizations that are not special. They will not move until they are convinced you are special like them. The moment you convince them, and they confirm it when they come work for you, your future candidate standard will skyrocket.

Why employee turnover
is the ultimate organizational disruptor

But there may still be a problem. You may still be where the monster wants you to be. He wants you to allow him to be a disruptor, just like Godzilla ripping up whole cities. You lay awake at night thinking "What am I going to do now?"

You just lost a key employee or an employee who you had plans for in the future. Or maybe you are just losing too many of the employees who make up the backbone of your company. In most cases, disrupting is a very negative thing.

How many times have you been in the middle of a project and a key player resigns? The project is completely disrupted and sometimes must either be delayed or abandoned. The cost can be calculated in expense; but, many times the opportunity lost can be in the millions of dollars.

Early in my career we had to learn quickly what the root causes of our turnover were and what needed to happen to stop the bleeding.

**90% of the corrective actions
had one thing in common - they were proactive**

In today's business world "disrupting" can be seen as a positive thing. To disrupt is to challenge conventional thinking. So much of what you are currently doing with your greatest asset is based in conventional thinking. Do more, do it quickly, pay more and spend more. How is it working out for you?

If conventional thinking is not producing the results you want, then it needs to be abandoned and you need to look at opportunities outside the box. We got out of the business of fighting fires and started building proactive strategies and systems. We did not allow the monster to disrupt our organization because we were always ahead of it.

One of the benefits which we received when we slayed the monster is that we had many of our competitors employees wanting to come work for us. We could cherry pick their employee for no more hourly rate then what they were making at our competitor's company.

They were not coming for the money. They were coming for a host of other reasons: respect, technical support, more hours, cross training and the ability to make a difference for a growing company.

The Dreaded Dance:
One step forward – two steps back

Currently you are having some success - the monster wants you to think so. He will give you a few hours of celebration before he pulls the rug out from under you.

Has this ever happened to you? You got him! He accepted the offer. This is a key position and it has been open for too long. You had to pay more than you wanted to but it will be worth it. You are celebrating, high fiving, planning the party.

Then one of your supervisors comes in and tells you one of his key people just quit. Before you even start talking about how hard it will be to replace him, another supervisor lets you know that one of his key people is also quitting.

The party never happens. You are worse off than when you started the day. This is how the monster works. One step forward – two steps back. How are you going to replace these two employees with their skills? You had real plans for one of them. Maybe you can save him by telling him what you were thinking. Your chances are slim to none.

The monster wants you demoralized and defeated

This is how the monster can drain and demoralize you and your organization. You think you have a small victory and then he hits you – HITS YOU HARD! What is the use of trying?

I remember how it was when I fought the monster the first time. Every day coming in and killing myself trying to save an employee while two slipped out before I could even respond. The root causes were in full bloom, yet I did recognize them, much less know what the solutions were. I remember thinking, "there has to be someone out there who knows what to do, how to do it and even more importantly what NOT to do."

It took so much time to figure it out. But once we did, it was exhilarating to learn how to fight back – HIT HIM HARD! We knew the symptoms, we had a plan and we fighting back. What a feeling! Not just fighting fires but knowing we had a plan.

What do you think it felt like when we scored some points – made some head way? When we knew we were hurting the monster? It felt awesome! Now, I wait for that moment when I know we have turned the tide. It is like watching a football game where one team is beating the other team really badly. Then the momentum shifts and the other team catches up and now you have a whole new game.

Skills Gap

The Third Head

Sell the vision – connect the dots – make the connection

Never forget that the employees who have desirable skills always have lots of options. The number and extent of their options will correspond directly to the demand for their skills. No doubt they are going to make good money and they will be able to a great extent make their own rules. They are special therefore they will be treated special. And trust me, they know it. You are feeding the monster when you get into a bidding war for a person with a desired set of skills. I walk away if I am interviewing a person who has a set of desired skills and they are all about the money.

They are friends with the monster and they use each other to get what they want

How do you solve this problem? I look to the organization for the solution. It is easier to sell more to an existing customer than find a new one. It is also easier to take the good employees you do have and make them great employees. Give them new skills and offer more opportunity. Have them increase their value to the organization.

Yes, there are pitfalls and you need to know how to identify and steer clear of them. The monster is in full control of the pitfalls and wants you to fall into them. Since the pitfalls are the work of the monster they are expensive and frustrating.

To begin with, how many of your employees really understand the strategic vision of your company? More importantly, do they understand how they can help make it happen? One of the first things I do when I start working with a company is to identify how many employees are in tune with either of these questions. What I have found is the vast majority of the employees do not.

The problem is that too many companies talk about vision and what it means to the organization. Great employees don't want to just know how it benefits the organization. They want to know how they can help make it happen and what it means to them. If you can connect the dots between what they are doing every day, how it helps the organization succeed and how they will benefit – you will supercharge your employees.

Pay raises for time served or enhanced value?

Most organizations provide for pay raises on what I call "Time Served". We all have seen these types of programs – after six months you will have an evaluation and an adjustment which is within a fairly tight range. What I have found is that great people are demotivated by time served compensation plans. Why? Time served plans are based on the lowest common denominator.

Great people, by nature, will increase their value much faster than the lowest common denominator. Do you remember back in school when the class was going much slower than the speed you could master the material? Bad employees are fine with time served plans because they ARE the lowest common denominator.

Pay differences between employees should reward and retain top performers and motivate all others

Great employees are motivated by value based plans because they can set their own timetable. However, they want to be compensated at the time of the value-add and not some artificial time-based program which has nothing in common with the timetable of their value increase.

This is corrected by having a value-based compensation program (Value Pathing) with objective criteria set by the company. The more you can show the path and the rewards the more the employees will stay with you.

If you can show the rewards will indeed be given when they achieve the objectives of the path, you will reinforce the need for them to continue walking the path. The employees who complete the path will be standing on a mountaintop which provides the pay, benefits and status which they desire and you need.

Too many times when I review the pay of an organization's employees, the spread between the Good to Great employees and the Average to Bad is not wide enough. The pay goal for the Good to Great is what they are truly worth to you.

For instance, when you lose a Good to Great employee and your first thought is you are going to have to pay more to replace him, you are missing something. Why would you be willing to pay someone you do not know more than an employee who works for you now? The pay goal for an Average to Bad employee is to motivate them to learn more, attain more experience and add value. You will then be able to pay them more. The last pay goal is to force out the truly bad employee.

The saddest example I ever witnessed was a 30-year employee who was greatly valued except in her pay. The owner said that they were concerned when this employee retired. "So much value, knowledge and experience will be leaving with her," he said. When I looked at the pay, she was barely making more than a new employee who had just been hired.

Structural Motivation and Value Pathing^{TM}

The monster is an expert at taking employees from you before they have been trained beyond the minimum needed to produce at the lowest level. How many times do you have to get involved in something because none of your employees have the ability to handle the issue?

This was the biggest problem we had the first time I fought the monster. Our senior technicians took years to train and acquire the necessary experience. It took them only moments to walk out the door.

This problem exists in every manufacturing and service company which I know. I see many organizations failing to retain their employees during the complete training period which will make them the valuable employees the organization needs.

We identified why our technicians left during the five years while they were in training - their value to us was actually rising faster than their pay raises because their pay raises were limited by static time periods. The following chart represents how this happened. Mid-way through the training period they would pass a company training class and soon after leave for a competitor offering $2-3 more an hour.

All that value and training lost and is now giving value to the competition. The competition had turned the awesome company training program into a competitive advantage for them. The competition realized all the value with none of the cost! This was corrected when we implemented a value based compensation program (Value Pathing) with objective criteria set by the company.

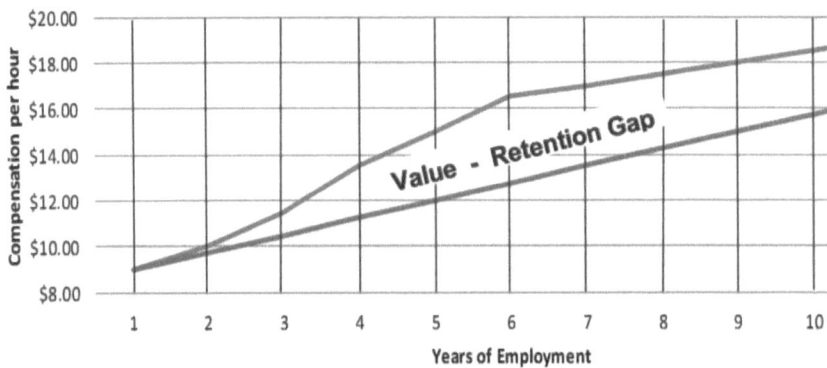

Once our compensation program matched the rising value of our employees, our competitor had nothing to offer. Turnover for senior technicians dropped significantly and was never an issue again. We were close to ZERO TURNOVER for our senior technicians.

The company is always in control of the path relating it directly to company goals

As time passed, I learned how this simple but complex concept could be used to structurally motivate employees both with money and other rewards. While most employees may not want structure, they need it and they want the long- term benefits of it.

The more you can show the path and the rewards the more the employees will stay with you. If you can show the rewards will indeed be given when they achieve the objectives of the path, you will reinforce the need to walk the path.

The employees who complete the path will be standing on a mountaintop which provides the pay, benefits and status which they desire and you need.

The mountaintop employees will reinforce the power of the path to the other employees

I have a theory about the makeup of our general workforce which has been borne out by Value Pathing™. Roughly 30% of our general workforce is made up of Great Employees. Great Employees have goals, will figure it out, make their own path and ultimately make it happen. We then have 10% of the workforce who are happy with government assistance. They make it clear they don't want to work.

This leaves about 60% of our workforce who want to work; but, do not fall into the Great Employee category. I call these people The Great Opportunity. Why? Because I have seen over and over these are the people who have the greatest change when they are impacted by Value Pathing™.

The members of the Great Opportunity generally have a higher degree of insecurities then the Great

Employees. They see themselves as not being able to do what the Great Employees do. They question whether they are smart enough, tough enough and have what it takes to be a Great Employee. What I have found is the answer to each of their questions is a resounding YES.

If you give them a Value Path as described above they will succeed. Why? Because it is the missing link they need to be a Great Employee. The real issue with the Great Opportunity members is that they have a hard time envisioning and developing the path on their own. But if you provide them with the Path and the opportunity to discover, they do have what it takes and they will become a Great Employee.

It is the Great Opportunity group which will have the greatest impact in your organization

There is one secret the monster does not want you to know. The Great Opportunity employees need the path more than the exceptional employees! When the Great Opportunity employees see the Great Employees at the mountaintop of the path, then the other employees who are at different stages of the path will engage the path.

The next step for the Great Opportunity employees is when they are successful in the beginning stages. They soon realize they can be successful. The employees who are using the value path are not limited in how fast they are moving forward. They are allowed to set their own rate of advancement within the requirements of the path. At this point you will see employees who are not just walking up the path but they are RUNNING! This was due strictly to the flexibility given by the value path and the desire of the employees to get to the mountaintop as quickly as possible.

This will ultimately reduce your training period. For instance, our training period was cut from five years to a little over two years. Just imagine the reduction in cost of training and the increase in revenues as you are able to put people with the skills they need out in the marketplace quicker. This also led to our employees incomes rising faster. Therefore, we were able to reduce our turnover while increasing revenues.

The ultimate goal of Value Pathing™ is increased productivity

What does every business owner want beyond a stable workforce? They want an efficient, productive workforce. They want less cost-per-dollar of revenue and a major component of cost is payroll. The ultimate goal and a consistent result of Value Pathing is this: fewer people making more money per person with a much higher level of revenue-per-dollar of payroll. You are setting an increased standard, providing a path for success, motivating and rewarding your higher performers and allowing the lower performers to move on.

Think about how you would feel if you were one of the successful employees. Would you feel valued? Would you feel loyalty? Would you tell your family and friends about your experience? What if you were someone being told this story by the employee? Would you want to know more about this employer?

The monster is REELING from the body shots

Why organizations resist turnover reduction

Don't be deceived. The monster lives in YOUR organization! A crazy thought isn't it? He lives there in the agendas and thought processes of your employees. But why would anyone be against lower turnover?

It's hard to believe, but every time I have helped someone with their turnover there are individual employees and groups of employees who are actively working against me in reducing the turnover. Let's look at a couple of these groups:

1. Bad employees
2. The people who are currently charged with reducing turnover
3. Middle management who may lose power with the new policies
4. Anyone else who feels threatened

Bad employees feed on your employee turnover. You can't get rid of bad employees as long as your turnover is out of control. As we all know, bad employees are the number one source of negativity in your organization. They will always be the first to determine what is wrong with anything you are doing and how it is bad for the employees. They are literally running off your better employees and this increases their power.

When you have a major reduction in employee turnover it makes the current responsible party look bad - especially if it is done in ways which were rejected by them in the past. The more your turnover is reduced, the more it makes them look bad and the more they will resist in one way or another.

Any new ideas, strategies and policies will be deemed to be wrong and "won't work here".

Do not underestimate the power of the monster in your organization

These individuals or groups will never come out and discuss the real reasons why they are opposed. They will always present a false impression of their concerns. Many times their concerns will be hidden behind a veil of "the good of the employees". The reality is their concerns are for their own self interests.

I have seen this many times, an organization stuck where they are with little to no progress being made. Any new ideas are evaluated not in an objective, "what is best for the company", way but in a veiled review of how it will affect the above captioned parties.

Many times a simple review of what they lose versus what they gain will blunt many of their concerns. You are playing to their very issue – their self-interests.

What have we learned?

The monster can be slayed! He is not invincible or as powerful as he wants you to believe. The root causes are different for every company. The strategies, plans and processes will also be different. Results vary but you will be better off by taking the monster straight on then continuing to let him ravage your organization.

Are you ready to slay your monster?

Clark A. Ingram

Phone: 405-508-1059

www.PeopleProfits.com

Clark.Ingram@PeopleProfits.com

www.ingramcontent.com/pod-product-compliance
Lightning Source LLC
Chambersburg PA
CBHW030847180526
45163CB00004B/1486